# MY ENCOUNTER WITH GOD AS A COMMERCIAL TRUCK DRIVER

by
EDWARD SMITH

Olympus Story House

To my Lord and Savior Jesus Christ:
I am persuaded that it was He who inspired me to share my testimonies and my encounters with Him so that these can be a witness of His love and care for us and ultimately allow us to share in His kingdom.

To my mom (now deceased):
Her example in steadfastness and commitment to complete any task she undertook. There were times during this project when I felt drained and exhausted, and I thought of taking a sabbatical, but as I recalled her spirit of commitment and dedication to her tasks, I was energized to move forward.

To my wife:
Through the long hours of many nights, she sacrificed her needed rest to engage me in the conversation for me to complete my late-night driving.

# CONTENTS

# ACKNOWLEDGMENT

This production is no means a reflection of any skill or talent possessed by me. Had it not been for the patience and skill of my family, this product would not have come to fruition. They not only constantly turn on the computer for me, but often before I retire, they made sure my last page was up and that everything was set for me to proceed during the early morning hours. Therefore, I acknowledge the support of my wife Delaine and my two daughters Nicola and Sherene, along with my grandson Keanu. In as much as I spent tiresome hours writing and joggling my memory to unearth my ability to use grammar and structure sentences, had it not been for the input of my other daughters, Dacialois and Atarah, who guided me through the difficult editing process, this project would not be so penetrating as it is. So a generous thank you to my family.

# INTRODUCTION

I was born and raised in a Christian family many years ago in Guyana, South America. Growing up, I was fascinated by outdoor life and hands-on activities that required physical dexterity and creativity to accomplish. Being the son of a preacher, I was exposed to numerous religious activities at an early age, so it was no surprise that I developed an interest in theological discourses very early in life.

I experienced the passing of my father in my mid to late teens. As a result, I relocated to an industrial region and sought employment to help my mother. It was during those years that my interest in commercial vehicles surfaced; I was fortunate to have had several jobs that required knowledge of driving. Little did I perceive that so many of my Adult Years will be spent as a commercial driver, appreciating the outdoors and beholding so much of nature while I traverse the highways. Almost all the testimonies mentioned in this book occurred outdoors. *Could it be that my early experience in hands-on activities and outdoor events must have been dormant, waiting for the opportune time and being the channel through which God will communicate with me?* He made us, we are His and He wants to stay connected with us, and He knows how to attract our attention individually.

I pray that as you read this book, for those who are currently walking with God, fasten your grip securely, and for those who are not yet on that journey that they will be inspired to join us and feel a connecting cord with God. He is pointing in a different direction and beckoning you saying, "I want to use you."

# I AM EVERYWHERE

As the preacher's kid, it was a standard practice that I attend every service of the church. In fact, up until age thirteen, church services were conducted in our house, and I was always in attendance. He (God) knew me before I was formed; He was setting the stage on which He will have me to stand and display Him before the universe. Through a series of circumstances, He brought me from New York to a previously little-known city in central Florida (reminiscent of my birthplace). My life in New York was very hectic. It was painfully challenging to coordinate my work activities and my family life. With my children's staggering school activities and being able to fulfill my role satisfactorily in church, leadership was very difficult at times and even overwhelming. There were days that I felt my functions were all ritualistic and mechanical. I longed for a free day so I can whisk my little ones away from the hustle of the metropolis. Without exaggeration, often when returning from an out-of-town trip, as we approached the city, there was a feeling in the atmosphere, a strange sense and awareness that we are almost back in New York. Our feeling of depression indicated that there was something in the atmosphere, sort of thick or heavy, but not quite able to articulate it here.

There was just too much of uneasiness. It was incumbent that I extracted my family from this contamination of the metropolis.

Over the course of one year, I dedicated several days of prayer and fasting, petitioning God honestly for direction as I considered relocating. When Florida came on the radar, I hinted my plans to a few in my congregation. Hearing that I have thoughts of relocating to Florida was distasteful to many. At that point, it was as though God had already channeled the response through them. They were all very aggressive, and some were very stern in their responses. Therefore, I choose not to solicit their prayers because they were ready to discredit my idea of relocating.

Then it dawned on me that it's not always necessary to share some dreams with certain ones. I could continue trusting God and was sure beyond the shadow of doubt that He (God) was leading.

# MY EARLY TEST

My initial visit to Florida in search of a house was not fruitful. Nevertheless, two weeks following that visit, I did something that was not popular, and it was not a typical business practice. My Realtor called to explain that they had found the house they thought I liked.

While still in New York, not having an idea about the neighborhood complexities and other factors that can impact our lives, no immediate concerns crossed my mind. Within a few days, I entered into a contract and made a deposit.

In less than thirty days, our household furniture and other belongings were all in a U-Haul headed southward. I was convinced that my move was designed by God. I continued trusting Him and was convinced beyond the shadow of a doubt that He was leading.

I was given an address to a title office to do closing. I had no clue what that meant. All I recalled now is that I met in the room with two or three individuals, spent almost two and a half hours, and signed several documents, after which I congratulated and departed for my new home with a set of keys. Before long, I was back in my U-Haul with an atlas, navigating my way to the property I had just bought.

By all of today's standards, my action and movement in acquiring that house would be considered irresponsible or perhaps senseless. Shortly after moving, I was faced with the challenge of adjusting from a busy New York life to a tranquil community. My delivery service in New York made provisions to compensate me on a weekly flat rate, regardless of the volume of production.

My contract in this Southern region was unlike what it had been in New York. The Florida contract provided for compensation based on the volume of service or work provided, in other words, no service rendered, no pay, minimum service rendered, minimum compensation, much services rendered, much compensation.

Considering now that I was committed to a monthly mortgage note to a financial institution, unlike previously where I was obligated to a landlord with whom I could have negotiated easily in the event of a financial set back, the Spirit reminded me that I had nothing to be worried about and He who started this good work in me will see me though to the end.

I sensed that the *Lord* wanted me to trust Him even when it doesn't seem to make sense. At the end of my first year in Florida, the company with whom I had the contract demanded that all contractors upgrade from box trucks to what is called over-the-road vehicles, meaning tractors and trailers (big trucks). Now I had only weeks to do a transition from the box truck to a semi.

A major conflict immediately erupted in my head, *Was it God's voice I had heard that led to my action the relocating? Was it His will that I was affiliated with this company? Or was He setting me up for a test?*

I knew absolutely nothing about combination vehicles. I was always uncomfortable traveling too closely to a semi, and now I was harnessed by an uneasy feelings internally.

I was not associated with anyone owning a commercial vehicle, and being relatively new in the area, I had not yet established any relationship with people qualified to guide me through this process of acquiring such an equipment. Not only was my credit score unacceptable, but I had no training on how to operate that vehicle. *So how was that mountain to be crossed? At times thoughts flashed across my mind, Should I retreat to my familiar circle, that is New York, among those who had cautioned me concerning my relocating plan? Should I contact my previous employer about returning?* My prayers were now in the form of a question, Lord what should I do? The scripture that came to my mind was in Luke 9:6, which says, "No one who puts a hand to the plow and looks back is fit for service in the kingdom of God." With these words from the Scriptures, I was energized to move forward on a journey with the Lord.

For seven days as I traveled back and forth to work, I parked on the shoulder of the road across from a commercial truck dealership and touched the fence as a point of contact, petitioning the Lord to bless me with a specific truck that I had identified at that dealership.

You need to know that at this time, a commercial driver's license (CDL) had just been introduced.

In my state, I was allowed to be grand fathered in by simply doing the written test. At the end of seven days, I was approved for a truck, which I did not know how to operate. I struggled to navigate my way home and to park the truck in my yard. I tossed all night battling with the question, *What have I done?* A truck was parked in my yard, and I had no clear path in moving forward. Jeremiah 32:27 was my verse of consolation. With that energy and inspiration derived from the Word, the Lord pointed me to a carrier.

I signed my contract and was ready for business. Orientation is a standard practice that precedes hiring, and mine was unique in that, I had never connected a tractor to a trailer nor had a pre-trip inspection. Yet I was commended by my prospective safety officer on my skillful maneuvers and test drive. (That was God)

# ALONE WITH GOD

When anything seems impossible, that's when I need to trust Him more. Over time, I was able to identify several churches where I can worship and spend the Sabbath while on the road. On this Friday afternoon, when I was unable to chart my course to one of these selected locations, I elected to spend the Sabbath at an unfamiliar truck stop but positioned myself in such a way that I may be free from distractions, as well as to be able to admire the mountain range.

After my morning devotions and having read a few chapters, I became restless. It was difficult to explain my emptiness, but it felt unfulfilling and strange to be alone on the Sabbath, especially during the hours that were structured for prayer and worship.

For all the previous years, I had been accustomed to having this experience within walls and as a part of our congregation, but now in solitude, with no one to share my worship experience as a custom for many years. Later in life, I attended numerous outdoor worship sessions, but those also were corporate.

I had been accustomed to worshiping Him in buildings made by hands. In those buildings, we speak of Him as having made all things, including nature. I was well familiar with the text in Psalm 19:1, "The heavens declare the glory of God, and the firmament shows His handiwork."

This scripture was indelible edged in my brain from youth, but now I was able to gaze at His majestic mountain, with streams of clear running water down through the valley, all because of His hands, yet at the same time feeling empty and restless.

Suddenly, a statement flashed across my mind. I heard a voice in my ear in the form of a question, *Can you see me? Can you see me though my work? Did you not sing of me. Oh Lord my God, when I in awesome wonder consider all the things your hands have made?*

I was now seized by a full awareness of His presence. All the bliss of my past worship experiences had faded away in insignificance; nothing was more dynamic that these one-on-one encounters with my Creator. It was not a moment to share in congregational worship; it was a moment exclusively with my Creator and me.

Imagine yourself in a huge building without any interior walls or furniture, and it is as dark as midnight, and then suddenly a loud voice calls you by name, and its echoes reverberate in a deafening tone. You know there is no way to escape, you feel overwhelmed and overpowered, and then you consciously decide to submit to the control of whatever or whomever the voice represents. Well, the moment I experienced the voice was not necessarily a frightening moment. I knew He wanted a one-on-one meeting with me. As we spent the remaining hours of the Sabbath, it was clear to me God wanted me to know Him at a different level. I needed a personal relationship with Him, and I was now hearing voices in my head, "You told me while within the walls, you told me you love my majestic creation, you acknowledge me and the grandeur of my world, right now I offer you to feel me and experience me at a different level."

You see my friend, I was not now in a structured worship service, guided by protocol, no song service, no praise and worship, no offering gathering time, no children's story. I know all the events leading up to the spoken word or what's often referred to as the eleven o'clock hour or divine service. You see, my problem was that

I had attended church services for so long that I had been a part of many planned services for many years all in a sanctuary and that had become a part of my life. I can be awakened in the middle of the night and plan a full day's church programs and execute them flawlessly. I recalled planning several *nature programs*. These activities were all conducted outside, explaining how God had made the trees and ordained their functions, even their roots, their trunk, and the tiny veins on each leaf— and the question was, I was confronted by those objects of nature made by the Creator, why am I not at peace, and why can't I feel His presence?

I felt like God was chipping away at the practice, customs, and protocols for the meetings, like a president in his office, patiently waiting on a private citizen for a one-on-one, no news media, no secret service, simple one-and-one. I felt that He had successfully released me from being bound by formality. He was instilling in me the hunger for a personal relationship. I do not intend to downplay the significance of assemblies or gatherings for worship. In fact, Jesus admonished that we do not forsake the assembling of ourselves together. However, for those experiences to be meaningful, it is imperative that we have a personal relationship with God.

My encounter at that moment strengthened my conviction of His interest in me. I was humbled and in awe by the reality of His presence. You are never alone, regardless of your past or your present situations. Whatever your doubts and your fears, whatever your peculiar circumstances are, please be assured He wants to spend time with you alone. I encourage you today, even if you must practice it during the midnight hours or anytime apart from your family worship time, to take ten minutes while in your car in the parking lot, commune with Him and feel Him in your spirit, you will experience Him, you will hear Him in such a way and will feel Him closer than you ever felt before, and your life will never be the same.

# ANGEL IN DISGUISE
## Part 1

He is all up in my business, I mentioned earlier, but I'll see the general rule prior to sunset on Friday. I began to assess the distance ahead and identify a local congregation that I can join for fellowship on the Sabbath. On this day, I was on a lengthy stretch of road with no city exit in sight, and those that I had passed were distant apart from each other.

It seemed likely that I might be spending the Sabbath *alone with God*. With my attention focused on finding an appropriate location, it was too late when I noticed that I had missed an exit. Looking somewhere that can possibly have accommodation. I was now more determined and hasted for the other exit rather than to turn back to what I had missed. However, upon exiting now, I noticed a fuel station with a convenience store along with parking accommodation. I secured a comfortable location where I can enjoy refreshments and rest. I was not aware that I was in for a counter with God and one that will strengthen the bond we had enjoyed earlier in a similar situation. I then did what was routine, worked my way up to the facility, and did my usual preparation. Returning to my truck, I realized I had locked the keys in with the engine on. I clenched my fist and stood frozen for a moment; confused, shattered, and bewildered words were inadequate to describe the moment. Law enforcement informs me that not only do they no longer can offer help to unlock commercial vehicles but there is no known locksmith road service in this small town. Painfully, I made my way to the store attendant explaining my plight and inquiring about the nearest mobile unit that can provide service. He gazed at me with amazement and then uttered the most painful words for the day, "Sorry," he mumbled in a low tone of voice, "there is no help for you in this town."

With a heavy heart, I labored my way to my truck speaking to God, "Lord, what have I found myself in today? How will you get me out of this? How will you pull this off?" Then negative thoughts raced violently like a whirlwind through my mind. Well it's all my fault. I should not have accepted this assignment after certain time on Friday. Now I must deal with the consequences. Whatever profit there was in this load was about to be affected by having to utilize the service emergency mobile company from another town. The multitude of negative thoughts that had clouded my mind was flushed out by an avalanche of words of hope—words such as "The angel of the Lord encamped around them that serve Him"; "All things work together for good to those who love the Lord and those who called by His name"; "When you go through the waters, Ill be with you, and when you go through the fires, you will not be burnt. Stand and see the salvation of the Lord"

Well, I thought of the call to Moses. When he questioned his ability to accomplish the task he was asked to perform, he let the Lord know that he was not equipped with what it took to fulfill the moment, all I had available to me or in my hands were a few pieces of broken wire from a nearby fence I thought I can use as a clothes hanger to unlock my door. With a song in my heart, I preceded the handle hoping to grab the component and accomplish my goal, I was attracted by the sound of a vehicle approaching me. This will help. I seized my operation and recognized that it was in a noncommercial mobile repair truck, and my spirit was lifted. I knew there was something he could do for me; he might be able to provide a lead.

"Was it you who called for service?" He inquired.

"No sir, it must have been the guy parked nearby, but he might have left." The conversation continued.

"So what are you doing?" He inquired.

And, in a monotone, I uttered, "Trying to get this door open." I can't recall any dialogue, but the next thing I knew is that he reached into his vehicle for his unlocking tool. My friend, this all occurred so quickly, so I thought it must have been a dream. Before I knew it, my door was unlocked, and he was on his way. I stood gazing and slightly dazed with no time to offer any payment or show any act of gratitude; he was completely out of my sight. After regaining composure, I made my way to the store attendant and inquired about the service vehicle that was on the premises. He was very empathetic in saying, no, sir. "Did he purchase fuel perhaps using his credit cards at the pump and not having to enter the store?" I inquired. "Could he have vanished unnoticed?" I stretched my memory to recall the features and even the color of the vehicle, but to this day, I cannot recall it. I recalled walking again to the truck and trying very hard to make sense of all that had just happened. While in my shock, I pondered on Genesis 18:1–3. I asked myself, "Is anything too hard for God" I believe that God has thousands of ways to fix our situations, and most of these ways we know not of. He wants us to know that He's always there for us and that we need to trust and depend on God. I had always been a conscientious and hardworking individual with regimented tendencies, very schedule oriented, and analytical. As a country boy, my mom raised me in a very disciplined life, my tomorrow's activities were all well planned and sorted out today, so success is assured as my plans are executed. Planning a trip to the city can be a once-a-year event; my mom would make sure that before we retire the previous night, all clothing is prepared and laid out in such a way as to avoid any delay on the day of the occasion. Everything that needs to be done on that trip must be with keen scrutiny, including every penny that needs to be spent. Well, nothing is inherently wrong with planning and strategizing, but it is important to recognize that God has the final say. He must manage you no matter how small the task or the project is, present it to God, and believe He will guide you in the execution of it. I was always obsessed with elaborate preparation; therefore as I grew older, I associated success in any endeavor with the ability to plan and to execute perfectly. In so doing, I sometimes leave no room for God in my affairs. In my quest for success, I was so wrapped up in strategizing and planning, but I was not in tune with the master of success. So through a series of events, such as the one I last mentioned, He taught me to depend only on Him for success. I have spoken to Him in spirit based on the things I needed, and He responded with a physical manifestation. But because I was caught up in the physical problem, lamenting my situation that when God was ready to respond, I was not in the channel to hear and understand Him. Why was it that I missed the planned location? Could it be that the one I ended on was more favorable for God to demonstrate to me how much He cares about me and that He is up in my business? With room only for a small number of semis, would it be easier for a small service vehicle to do what needs to be done? In my humanity, I often struggle to grasp the purpose of the divine. I acknowledge that plan and preparation have their places, but the Lord, I believe, was working on me. He was systematically and deliberately shedding stuff off from me to prepare me for future duties. With too many of my strategies, my plans, and my game, He must shave and carve to fit me in the position He has for me, but during the pain, Paul reminds me that God's grace is sufficient for me.

Dear reader, God wants to be all up in our business. He's trying to set us up for His purpose. I encourage you to be in tune with Him and to be sure His spirit is connected to yours, and I promise you, your life will never be the same. Psalm 34:7 says, "The Angel of the Lord encampeth round about them that fear Him." I've made that my frequent quotation for consolation.

# ANGEL AT THE HELM
## Part 1

Most of the commodity I transport is refrigerated and therefore very time-sensitive. It was not unusual for me to commit to a load to be delivered one thousand miles away and be told that the merchandise was already scheduled for distribution. In some cases, the product was already advertised as available for the consumers. With that pressure on any carrier, especially when there is a fine associated with late delivery loss of sales, a driver must push himself to accomplish that feat. It was a normal day. I had accomplished my routine walk around inspection as required by the department of transportation. But beyond that, I am of the practice of laying hands on my semi including all eighteen tires as well as my steering wheel. Every mile of the way, I am conscious of the presence of my angel, yes, especially in the night hours when there is less distraction around. One hundred percent of my attention is required at nights because most of my friends and relatives are unavailable for communication that will keep my mind active, hence 100 percent dependence on my angels. I recalled one night, darkness had just crept in. I had been nourishing my soul with spiritual songs and reflecting on how God had been so good to me but pause to pay my bridge toll. I recalled having the toll receipts in my hands and attempting to adjust myself preparing the make my way over a four-and-a-half-mile-long bridge across a lake. The next moment of consciousness was a feeling of freezing wind on my face. Now being fully conscious, I was trying to make sense of what had just taken place. Not knowing where I was and trying to stay calm enough and in control, I realized I had been holding my change from a toll plaza as well as my receipt. For a quick few seconds, I felt something rush through my body, a feeling I still cannot explain. I had slept my way across the bridge, and I had driven another three miles on the road surface before crossing a second bridge a half mile long. After having crossed the second bridge, I drove another five to six miles on the road surface on a three-lane highway exited, stopped at the green light off the ramp, and paused for a moment. It was a cold and dark winter night well after midnight, and apart from the traffic light on the interstate, there was literally nothing that suggested that life was around. The thought of what had just happened traumatized me beyond what I cared to explain. I had been hauling approximately seventy-five thousand pounds of combined weight, it's very torturing and traumatic to think that I was oblivious to my surroundings when I had navigated my way on a two-lane bridge, that is constructed with a seventy-five percent degree turn at center span. Not only was I at risk of plunging into the depths of the lake but taking along with me any number of innocent vehicles. What led me to exit the interstate stopped at the red light and extend my hands to open my door for an exit is inexplicable to this day. Why had I stopped at that light and why had I been trying to exit the vehicle are all unanswered questions. After regaining consciousness, I remained in that position for several seconds before I proceeded to a safe haven for several hours; the more I reflected on what had just occurred, the more difficult it was for me to continue my journey. With a ranging mind and a trembling body, I was unable to induce sleep, also too troubled to drive. I don't quite recall the duration of time I spent at that location, but I did finally make it to my destination. How could I quit repeating "The angels of the Lord encamped around about those who fear Him"? I don't know whether it was my angel that held the wheel for those moments that I slept or might have been Jesus Himself who kept me in my lane or changed lanes for me, but this one thing I know; my God never sleeps or slumber. I ask God time and time again, "What is it that I have yet to do for you? You have a destiny for me. You constantly, miraculously bring me through these situations. Why are you still delivering me from this?" I can truly exclaim! Taste and see that the Lord is good; blessed is a man who trusts in Him. Isaiah told me, "Though I go through the waters, it will not overflow me. Although I go through the fire, I will not be burned. My covenant will I not break nor alter the thing that is gone out of my lips. I know that my Redeemer lives." These are not words I am just reporting or reciting, but these experiences have been real in my life, and that's the reason I feel compelled, energized, and brave enough to share them with you. God is real. Oh, taste and see that the Lord is good; blessed is the man who trusts in Him.

# INTERCEDING FOR OTHERS
## Part 1

My mind goes back to a rainy night in a Midwestern state. I had been doing my best to be safe during a torrential storm; therefore, I had adjusted my speed and positioned my truck in the extreme right lane referred to as the granny lane. I cannot account for any time, but the next thing I knew is that I was literally stopped in the soft dirt in the center medium. I had crossed all lanes on my left past the left shoulder and ended up where I was. Once again, sat frozen for a moment attempting to make sense of what had happened and being tortured by the thought of what might have happened while crossing those lanes. *Who was it that guided the vehicle, or perchance traffic just happened to be light or was delayed, or maybe traffic went ahead of me so rapidly that no one was around me when this occurred?* I wondered also if it had not gotten stuck in the mud and would have crossed the oncoming traffic, but worst yet, if the center medium was divided by a concrete barrier, my impact would have been devastating. By now I had become fully aware of my surroundings and was thanking God for the fact I was still on all eighteen wheels. I had no injury, and neither did I cause to hurt anyone.

It seems like no matter how devastating our situations are, there's always something for which we can be thankful. I thank the Lord that He was helping me to understand that He needs me around to accomplish something for Him. Thank you, Lord, for demonstrating that you never sleep nor slumber. I believe that at times the Lord brings such deliverance as a result of others interceding for us. My prayer partners are always actively interceding with God on my behalf, and there's no doubt in my mind that there's a benefit in having others petitioning our father on our behalf. Prayer partners are like watchmen on the wall who sleep not day nor night.

I am a part of a nationwide prayer line that operates 24-7. Many nights it's served as an anchor to my soul as I rolled down the asphalt. Songs testimonies, praise reports, and exhortations are always very uplifting. There was a particularly early morning moderator well known for her all-inclusive petitions. She would make a special effort to lift all travelers by air, sea or land.

Not only for the passengers but for the one at the helm. I felt a surge of energy rushing through my tired body as she petitioned in my behalf, "Lord, protect all those  big truck drivers," and my response is always "Thank you, Lord." It was not unusual to hear many of the prayers mentioning me by name, "Lord, be with Bro Smith  wherever he might be now."

# INTERCEDING FOR OTHERS
## Part 2

One morning between 4:00 a.m. and 5:00 a.m., she mentioned, "Lord, we have not heard from Bro Smith on this line for quite a few days now, but please continue to be with him." I accepted those prayers in my behalf and thank God for them. Later that very day shortly after noon, the brilliant sunshine was penetrating the heavens over the state of Arizona. I was reflecting on the wonders of creation as I took a quick glance at the towering mountains that flanked the interstate . I cannot account for what had happened in that split second, but the next thing I knew is that I was too close to the rear bumper of the commercial vehicle directly ahead of me and too close to brake to avoid a collision. I can only impulsively take a quick right dash without considering traffic in the right lane. After such a close and counter in the wild and risky perhaps even reckless maneuver, I exclaimed, "Thank you, Lord!" As I mentioned earlier, before the break of dawn, I had heard the prayer line coordinator mentioning my name, petitioning the Lord to cover me on my journey. Do I need to make more emphasis on the benefits of intercessory prayer, I am persuaded that more prayers are directed to the throne of grace on our behalf than we send for ourselves.

Truth be told, most Christians pray only twice per day, at night when they retire and then in the morning when they rise. One godly man said, "Pray without ceasing," and another inspirational writer puts it thus: "Prayer is the breath of the soul. It is the secret of spiritual power. No other means of grace can be substituted, and the health of the soul be preserved." For the remaining working hours, I was fully alert and energized, offering uninterrupted praise and worship to my savior. He never sleeps nor slumbers.

# INTERCEDING FOR OTHERS
## Part 3

Yet another mind-boggling encounter. It was a rainy night, and after navigating my way through that treacherous condition on the interstate, I had finally made my way to Brooklyn when my truck module became disabled. Fortunately, it was not very distant from my destination, so I decided to linger until daybreak. Those of you familiar with the borrow of Brooklyn can understand what it is like to have a disabled vehicle on the streets during the morning rush hour. The first question that came to mind was, Lord, why me? My carnal mind ran to and fro, fearing the worst; that is, law enforcement will demand that I be towed. For such a service especially requested not within regular working hours, the cost could be prohibitive, perhaps more than what I would have invoiced for the load being transported. In the midst of the distress, I was able to mumble the words, "Lord, help me," and then it suddenly occurred to me that one of my mechanic friends who can address this situation was residing in Brooklyn, not wanting to disturb him before 5:00 a.m. I decided to wait for daybreak, praying that I would not be forced to move, and then the Spirit reminded me of the ever-present twenty-four-hour prayer line in

Brooklyn. After being on that prayer line for less than ten minutes with my phone on mute, I felt thrills down my spine when (the late) Sister Carol mentioned me in her prayers, Lord, remember those truck drivers including Brother Smith. He hasn't been on the line for two days, but wherever he is, be with him, amen. Having heard those words, my spirit was ignited with faith, hope, courage, and confidence to the extent that something rocketed me from my seat and convinced me that I do not need to wait on anyone at daybreak, but God will take care of me right now. In the rain, I grabbed my umbrella, and with my flashlight tucked under one arm and my tools in the other arm, I whispered a prayer that God will help me to identify the problem. It might be simplistic for me to say to you that God is a mechanic. While in churches you sing, he's a doctor in the sick room, he's a lawyer in the courtroom, but have you ever been to the courtroom accused of something, or do we simply repeat the words of the song we enjoy when our spirits are down? Well, this one thing I know is that I have the liberty to add one line to that famous song and that is He's a mechanic on the road in times of trouble. As I gazed at that huge diesel engine with a prayer in my heart, bearing in mind the fact that I just heard someone petitioned him in my behalf, immediately I identified the problem; and within moments, I was able to resolve it, put away my umbrella, secure my tools, and as we say in the trucking world, (head on down the road. I mentioned earlier how passionate I am about being strategic and structured and that my success clearly depends upon that. Very often, the Lord reminds me that it's not about me and my ability to get things accomplished, that although I have introduced him in my situation earlier, it was the intercessory prayer of my prayer line family that caused Him to take charge of my problems and override my agenda. Indeed, we are our brother's keeper, and we must open our hearts and mention the names of others when we pray, lifting them up to the throne. Often, we are unaware of the difficulties and tremendous challenges that many are faced with. Therefore, we should not be selfish and limit our prayers for ourselves and families only; let's also extend them to accommodate others. Some pray,. Lord, me, my wife, and two kids, us four and no more. There are those who are sometimes pressed by life's burden and are wrestling with things beyond their ability to resolve. We need to make it our habit to include at least one person when we pray, petitioning in their behalf, for we are all connected by the cord of human brotherhood. I'm encouraged, and I'm encouraging you to minister to others and experienced the blessing that God has for you.

# ANGEL IN DISGUISE
## Part 2

He is a very present help in times of trouble. Thank God He never sleeps nor slumbers because it seems that it's mainly at night that most of my dramatic encounters occur. I had not too long ago entered the interstate when I notice a significant loss of air needed for the safe operation of my vehicle. I whispered a prayer and was able to position the truck at the shoulder of an exit and, sat wondering how single-handedly I would be able to undertake this repair. Very quickly I realized that I had not been parked completely off the road and that the air tanks were all totally empty, rendering the vehicle inoperable. In a matter of minutes, I was under the hood with the flashlights in one hand and tools in the other and proceeded to identify the problem. Time was against me due to my improper parking and the thick darkness looming in the skies; the task had become increasingly challenging. In a moment, my worst fear was realized, the sounds of a siren followed by flashing lights, and the state trooper had arrived. I already knew that it wouldn't be long before a wrecker would be summoned to take me away. Well, indeed, the trooper had arrived and beckoned me to his vehicle. I composed myself quickly and with a distressed look on my face, and a cracking voice, I proceeded to the officer's car offering an explanation concerning my plight. I assured him that my work can be done with dispatch, and before long, I will be on my way. In my haste, I had forgotten to display my triangles or my flasher to warn traffic of my improper parking. While talking to the officer, I had been praying that he would grant me grace and favor. I continued to explain that I knew exactly what needed to be done and assured him that in about thirty minutes, I will be gone. I tried to convince him about how committed I was, and before he was able to respond or utter a word, I proceeded to conduct my repairs. From the side of my eyes, I could see him on his radio talking to someone describing my truck and naming the exit where I was. In less than three minutes, a second trooper had arrived and parked behind me with emergency lights on. I had now begun to be overwhelmed and nervous; at that very moment, the troop that had first arrived politely offered to help me by using his highly luminous flashlight, and demonstrated such level of understanding, kindness, and courtesy. It was unbelievable!. Both officers tarried with me, one voluntarily held his flashlight so that I might perform the repairs, while the other returned to his vehicle and proceeded to use his traffic cone and triangles, positioning them on the road so that the oncoming vehicles will be aware of my disabled status. At the end of the drama, I realized that what seemed forbidding was really a blessing in disguise. When I recognized the second trooper, I was almost paralyzed by fear, but in fact, he was summoned by the first officer to offer me additional protection. I wondered, Why is it that my mind is prone to assume the negative first? Why did fear first subdue me before I call on God? Why did I quickly assume the worst at the arrival of each of the officers? At the break of day, when we commit ourselves to the Lord, do we not expect Him to take care of everything? Can it be that our prayers and request are simply rituals, or are we just into the formulation and meaningless practices? For as long as we have been walking with Jesus, should we not have already come to grips with Romans 8:28, which says all things, not certain things or some things but all things, finally work together for good to those who love the Lord and who are called by His name. For example, you are the most loyal and dedicated employee, and at the end of the day, a long day and difficult day, your supervisor invites you to his office and presents you with the infamous pink slip. Imagine the uproar from then on, the worst thought that dominates your mind, and the adjectives you use to label him or her. Is it worth it to be a loyal worker? Why me? Now he has placed my family in jeopardy. When will we come to the place in our lives and in our walk with God where we can respond to such a situation with a thank you, knowing that the Lord has something of greater value ready to wrap around us? "Yes, Lord," that's how I want it to be with my walk with God, to come to the place where I can say in a response to my employer, "Thank you, sir. This means the Lord has something better for me." I want to come to the place where if such a thing occurs in my life, I can sing on my way home thanking God and greet my family with honey. The Lord has opened a door with greater opportunities for me, and now our family can enjoy some of the things we always wanted. When we are prone to begin a pity party to question if God is on our side, we are quick to query, Is this my Jesus, or do I look for another? For me, that was a great lesson.

It reminded me that God can cause the sun to stand still until my victory is realized. That He can turn what seems to be a stumbling block into a stepping stone. My friend David said, "Oh, taste and see that the Lord is good." But I think of how often I have seen and experienced the grace and goodness of my God, and I still lack sometimes when it comes to being able to display spontaneous and positive reactions to certain situations. I am willing to acknowledge that it seemed like I have an intellectual understanding or a basic knowledge of what complete trust and confidence are, but it's not deep in my spirit to where I live fully. If I had been more in tune with the Spirit, it might have dawned on me to request the names, badge numbers, or unit numbers of those two officers who offered such a service to me. Why couldn't I think that they were simply angels that were sent to protect me rather than to think the worst (negative)?

My journey becomes usually much less stressful when I acknowledge that the Angel of the Lord encamps around me. There were times when I realized that something needed to be fixed but could trust Him to keep it going until I identify a safe location, and because I am aware of His presence or the presence of my angels, my courage is buoyed. It's one thing to know intellectually that my God shall supply all my needs, yet how quickly do I complain just as soon as I counter the simplest challenge?

# HE CONTROLS YOUR AGENDA

I was reflecting on that late afternoon as I was conducting a routine walk around my truck. I noticed a loose nut on my brake chamber. I gave thanks for that discovery because the darkness was approaching, and I had no plans to stop for the next several hours. I took a few moments to torque it correctly and was on my way. I had driven for less than two hours, and then my eyelids became heavy. It was not my agenda to stop that early, but my energy level had dropped suddenly, which necessitated a premature stop. I was disappointed about having to stop so quickly; it was disruptive to my agenda. At daybreak, I experienced another miracle. The nut that I had tightened securely was once again missing completely from the position. What went wrong? Did I cross- thread that nut? What could I have done to contribute to that loss of it? I had decided not to panic or to be spontaneously negative as in previous occasions nor allow my carnal mind to dominate; therefore, I positioned myself so I can examine the area to determine what might have been responsible for this frequent and usual backing off and ultimately loss of this nut. I was amazed, shocked, and speechless by this discovery. To those of you who can visualize a

tractor connected to a trailer at that position, the landing gear of
the trailer is near the rear wheel of the tractor. There is a flat base
at the bottom end of the landing gear, and on that plate was a
nut exactly the size of the one I needed to replace on my tractor.
I know this is not logical, but could it be that the missing nut
vibrated its way off and landed on the plate? Ridiculous. I conjure
thoughts and create scenarios in my head trying to justify the
discovery of this nut at that location. Could it be that some time
previously I had done some repairs of some sort and may have
forgotten an identical nut there? My mind raced back and forth
seeking a rational explanation for this phenomenon. Having gone
through several truck washes, truck centers, and repair shops where
the use of air pressure is required, it's hard to understand how a
nut can remain in that position for any length of time. Knowing
now that I have no reasonable or rational explanation for this
discovery, I proceeded to praise the Lord while oblivious to my
surroundings. I was now doing a Jericho walk while praising him.
I was simply thanking the Lord and spending the few remaining
hours contemplating how God wants to do so much more for me,
indeed for us. God wants us to have a relationship with Him to
ponder on His love and care for us, and that He who has given His
son to die for us can supply more than a piece of hardware for us
even when it seems impossible. Why did I become sleepy at the
time I did? And at that location, was that a coincidence, or was it
the Lord teaching me a lesson? In Romans 8:28, it was made clear
to me that He wanted to remind me that the angels of the Lord
encamp around those who fear Him. In that experience, I tasted
the goodness of God, not only when I asked Him to be with me
as a companion on my journey but that He who began this good
work in me wanted to see it through to the end. I realized He
wanted to remind me that He's not only at my point of pick up
as well as my point of delivery but that He is with me constantly.
I have come to the point where I learn how much to appreciate
God's involvement in the coordination of my work, as well as my
driving on a regular basis. I thank Him because when I need to
make a left turn, my mind is not confused and caused my hand to

do a left turn, and I thank Him that when I need the brake pedal, my mind and my body are in proper coordination to where I do not engage the gas pedal when I need this stop, nor do I step on the brake pedal when I want to gas it—these are simple things that we overlook, but I've learned to praise God for everything, having seen His goodness and His love for me. Apostle Paul puts it this way, in Him I live and move and have my being, for me to walk is Christ, to talk is Christ, to drive is Christ, to stop and deliver is Christ, everything about me is Christ. As Psalms chapter 91 says, He will give His angels charge over me. Is that protection limited to me as an individual, as a person, or is it extended to your property, your personal belonging? I subscribe to the idea that He covers both me and everything that carries my name. Once I was responding to several mothers who expressed deep concerns about their teenage boys' behavior. They had become rebellious and caused pain. I suggested to these mothers that while these young people were away from home, they can lay hands on their belongings, their pillows, their beds, their closet, and their footwear. Test the Holy Ghost, and speak blessings and power on their belongings so as they are dressed in their prayed-up garment, and as they walk, they will not be able to resist the working of the Holy Spirit in their lives. Little did I realize that I was in for a strong rebuke. All except one who was not a mother made it clear to me that scripture is emphatic and unambiguous regarding the laying of hands. They claim elders and pastors are the only ones to whom such function is assigned. They were amazed to hear that I frequently walk around my truck and lay hands on my wheels, my tires, my brake pedal, my steering wheel, and every moving part of my truck. I did not dispute them but allowed them to grow in the Lord, for indeed sometimes silence is golden.

# ANGELS AT THE HELM
## Part 2

I draw your attention to an early morning experience with my truck. I had set my engine to idle and return to my house gathering my personal belongings to leave. Returning to my semi after ten to fifteen minutes, I noticed it was moved from where it was left idling. Had someone stolen my idling truck? Were they in a hideout for me? Fear and trepidation gripped me almost to a paralyzing state, and adrenaline rushed violently through my system. I noticed at a distance, about two houses down the street, my vehicle was parked and still idling. I nervously made my way to it and realized that it had stopped at the entrance of a neighbor who had often shown her displeasure at my presence in that neighborhood; in fact, it stopped inches away from the bumper. Tremblingly, I reached for the door and was able to drag myself up into the cab and successfully removed my truck from being that close to my disgruntled neighbor's vehicle. To this day, I cannot fully explain that phenomenon. As much as my truck was in idling mode, never did it disturb the neighbor or cause any stir. Lord, why did the noise not wake that family? Why did it stop rolling just inches away, but most of all why did this occur with my unfriendly neighbor since it passed the vehicle of my friendly neighbor? Additionally, they usually walk their dogs in that time frame of the incident, but on that day, they did not. Whatever it was, I know that my God had His hands on my vehicle and so unlike my sister that rebuked me, believing that it is inappropriate to lay hands on anything apart from a body. May I remind you my friends that the whole world is sick, the environment is sick, your boss is sick, you are sick, and everything can benefit from the laying of hands.

Therefore, I am safe when I lay my hands on my truck and ask God to reveal His presence wherever I travel, and that's what kept me through these years. That incident occurred several years ago but it is still fresh in my memory.

# ANGELS AT THE HELM
## Part 3

One day I entered the fuel aisle to drop a package in the mail. I had shut the engine off and kept my feet on the break but had forgotten to apply the parking brakes. I exited the truck and quickly attempted to deposit the mail, but upon my return, I noticed my truck was missing. My mind raised trying to recall if I had been standing at the correct fuel pump, but as I saw a line of people moving swiftly in one direction, I recognized the gathering was around my jackknifed vehicle. The amazing report was that they saw my vehicle reversing at a slow-paced heading to collide with another parked truck, but it suddenly turned sharp enough to jackknife and lined itself back-to-back with another parked trailer, which resulted only in minor scratches. I mentioned earlier that my kind Christian female friends thought it was not appropriate to lay hands on the property but only on human beings; in my experiences, I can attest to that. My deliverances and all these miraculous maneuvers were because I had always exercised faith and trusted the Lord for the protection of these vehicles on which I laid hands on many occasions. Sometimes I reflect on those occasions, and questions still come to my mind, Why was it that while the vehicle was backing down the aisle, aiming for a collision with the truck that was in a designated spot, it suddenly changed the course and ended up the way it did? Each incident occurred several years ago, but as I chronicle it now, I'm still experiencing a strange inexplicable feeling within as I try to visualize or revisit the scene. Oh, for a thousand tongues to sing the great Redeemer's praise. My God can deliver not only me but my vehicle even when I'm not at the wheel. Some repeat the lyrics. He is a lawyer in the courtroom, but have they ever been subpoenaed before a judge? He is a doctor in a sick room, have they ever experienced a major surgery or had a loved one whose heart had stopped pumping for a considerable time?

I can add to that list and declare He's a driver in a big truck. He knows what exit to take while I'm sleeping;, the earth is the Lord's and the fullness thereof. When I take my truck to the shop, depending on the nature of the repair, they would allow me to wait for a specific day and to provide me with a technician who is disciplined and trained for the particular repair that needs to be done, but I know for my experience that my God is not skilled in a specific discipline. He created them all because He guided me through all of my repairs every phase of it. I need not wait on a specific time for Him to conduct it.

# THE STRENGTH OF AN ANGEL

Have you ever wondered how powerful an angel is, or better yet, can you imagine how your guardian angels relate to you? Your guardian angel is assigned to you and will always shield you in any dire situation. One day I had disconnected my trailer while being loaded., I, therefore, took the opportunity to complete a shopping errand, and upon return, I was advised to hook up my trailer and leave the dock. After obtaining my shipping documents, I reconnected my tractor and made my way to the exit point of the facilities. Before long I was headed for the street when I was alerted by a severe impact. Exiting the vehicle, I noticed the trailer's main connecting pin was released; the loaded trailer was resting on the chassis and not on the fifth wheel. It was my first experience of such, and my facial expression was obvious to the drivers standing nearby who of course rushed to my rescue. I had not perfectly hooked up the tractor to the trailer, and the extent of the damages could have been exorbitant, but with the cooperation of the drivers standing by, in a very short moment, I was able to reconnect without suffering any losses and was ready to continue my journey. But the most startling thing about this incident was the account a bystander. I had parked for a moment allowing myself to calm my mind from the trauma when a gentleman approached me and shared how breathtaking it was for him to witness the event. He explained that the trailer was already in motion to tilt to the right but suddenly changed its course and returned to its upright position. He was expecting the truck or trailer to overturn. It was like a movie in slow motion.

I sat there even longer and allowed it to marinate in my spirit. *How did God pull this off? Did He send the Red Sea strong wind, or did He commission angels that excel in strength to reposition my falling trailer with forty-five thousand pounds?. If so, how quickly did He summon them considering their response time, the distance between my location, and where they might have been at the time of their being summoned?* My thoughts or my questions might sound simple or humorous, but strange thoughts come to my mind after these experiences. *Why am I trying to figure out God? Can I, by searching, figure Him out?* There were many before my era who tried to figure out God, and His questions to them were, Where were you when I placed the moon, the sun, and the host of celestial bodies in the sky? In fact, I don't know how to explain how my brain communicates with my hands, my feet, and all the moving parts of my body, and I've been using these body parts for years and don't know how to explain them and how they function. It seems foolish, therefore, to spend time sorting out how He takes care of so many of us at the same time including capturing a forty-two thousand pounds trailer and stabilizing it before it topples to the ground. I can't fathom the Lord and can't explain Him. He is too great to be comprehended, but he's real. He is my protector, my provider, my driver, my helper, and my all in all. He deserves all my praise, and as David said, let everything that has breath praise the Lord.

Feel free to think that I am over exuberant or over animated or even completely out of my mind, but I want to say let the steering wheel praise the Lord, all rims and tires praise the Lord, tractor and trailer praise the Lord, and every moving part praise the Lord. When I first heard someone say let's give God some crazy praise,

I thought it was simply for the sake of entertainment. But from my experience when I speak of giving God some crazy praise you might think I am crazy, but I know why sometimes people do throw up their hands and run up and down the aisle. I was raised in a Christian community that would describe God as not the author of confusion. I read of a man who was lame all of his life, and he was healed by the master himself. The record says after he was healed, he was leaping. My friends, no one had to tell him how to express his praise and dance; the record said he was leaping for joy and made his way immediately into the house of worship, leaping into the church that must have been some crazy praise. When I think of the goodness of Jesus and all that He has done for me, my heart truly cries out, Hallelujah, thank God for saving me. I say that not because I simply want the quote words of a chorus or song but because that's truly the sentiments of my heart.

# HOLDING ON TO
# MY STUBBORN WILL

Thinking about all the huge stuff that He has fixed for me, the challenges, I exclaim, "Is anything too hard for God?" For a number of times and through the years, He has fixed so much for me, and He is still fixing in fact, and He had been fixing this tiny part for decades now. He has been prompting me to totally give up my heart so that He can exchange it for a new one. The delay is not due to Him; it's not His inability to perform the change, but it's on me. My brain, the seat of thinking often referred to as the heart, continues to cause challenges for me. I was stopped one day by law enforcement, and as I recall, the stop was unwarranted. Immediately that little me in me, that little man whom I thought was crucified, instantly was resurrected and was ready for defense. I saw the officer approaching, and I deliberately kept my window up as he drew near. I kept looking for him from the right, as if I was expecting him to approach me from the right, knowing fully well that he was in fact approaching me from the left. I kept that posture so that he would not think that I was ignoring him, but in fact I was. The little man in me kept on pushing vigorously and with tenacity, insisting that he remain in control. By now the officers suspected, but I had been ignoring him. He then banged on my door, but by now, that little man in me was mature, fully ignited, and steamed up for a battle. I was bold enough to query. (Why did he bang on my door?) It was now obvious that we were both ready to go at each other. He strongly requested that I meet him at his vehicle. Normally an officer gives a reason we are being stopped, but on this occasion, he did not. Instead, he requested my documents and then proceeded to his car. It's important that I share this with you in detail. You need to see what God accomplishes here. Now, remember he asked me to meet him at his vehicle. I deliberately delayed supposing, but I had difficulty gathering my documents. They were already at my hand reach then, but when I finally chose to approach him, my steps were as slow as can be, stopping frequently to re arrange the papers he had requested. I had almost reached the officer when the little man in me prompted me not to relent in my act. I stopped and shuffled the documents pretending that I had forgotten something in my truck. I made an about-turn heading back to the truck. Before I reached the door, here again I pretended that I had found the documents and did another about-turn leading toward him. By now you would think that the little man in me had won the battle and was satisfied with his victory. The officer took my documents and ordered me to go sit in my truck; that was when the inner battle escalated to a new height. Now I'm hearing voices in my head, How dare he order you to sit? Is he your mama? Could he not have been more polite and respectful?. I was now determined on showing full resistance to authority. I purposely and slowly proceeded to walk around my trailer, pretending I was doing a routine inspection. The inner man was in total defiance and void of reasoning and determined to maintain being in control, and he did not cease. Now finally I had made all my own necessary stops touching and examining things needlessly, cleaning my mirror, etc. Then I reluctantly entered my vehicle. Ladies and gentlemen, almost immediately after I sat, something marvelous transpired, and it was humbling to pen it with clarity. My moments of folly flash before me as in a panoramic movie. I never imagine that I had such a portion of stubbornness within. That acknowledgment led to crippling guilt and shame. I buried my head in the palm of my hands and bent forward on my steering wheel. I realized that I had taken the name of the Lord in vain., I had misrepresented Him as a Christian, allowing the old man whom I thought was crucified, to be resurrected and took full control of me for those moments. With a contrite heart and a broken spirit, I sought Jesus. In humility, I took responsibility for my foolishness and asked for forgiveness. I felt the peace as well as relief. I recalled the text that reads, thus, "If my people who are called by my name shall humble themselves .... I fully accepted his forgiveness and committed that old man once again to be crucified." Within moments, I heard a slight knocking on my door. Oh, how I wish I had someone to share this moment with. I wish you were there to witness the scene where the atmosphere was completely different.

With a very calm and respectful tone of voice, he called, "Sir,"and pleasantly staring into my eyes said the following words, "Hello, driver! I don't know why I'm doing this. I will not write you a ticket, just have a nice day." Ladies and gentlemen, that was a spirit-filled moment, that was truly a one-on-one encounter with God. Those moments are riveted indelibly in my spirit and my consciousness. I was sinking deep in sin, far from a peaceful shore, sinking very deep within, never to rise anymore, but the master of the sea heard my despairing cry and from the waters lifted me. Now, safe am I.

The old man whom I thought was buried had risen his ugly head and was in control of my life. He wanted to knock me down for the count, but someone told me that when the enemy comes in like a flood, then my God will lift a standard. God says He will never leave me nor forsake me, especially at a time when I am being pursued relentlessly by the devil. His ministering angel will not only steer a truck and guide in the repair process, but they will fight vigorously to save from sin and foolishness. I came to realize later, that the time I had been confessing my folly and my sins and entreating for forgiveness, the Holy Spirit had been touching the heart of the officer. Proverbs 2:1 says, "The LORD has the heart of the king in His hands, and He turns it wheresoever He wishes." I can't remember how long I tarried at that location, but this I know I will never forget those life-changing moments, those encounters, and how encouraging it was to allow Jesus to lead and defeat the enemy. The battle with self was intense; the self was relentless in pursuit, but my Jesus prevailed. Amen.

I'm here to assure you that no matter how fierce the battle of self is, no matter how ominous it seems, your victory is sure. Don't think you will overcome Him through self-discipline alone. The apostle dealt with this too; he said he knew what he wanted to do and what not to do but was in struggle to perform it. He cried out for deliverance, but he announced that he had gotten the victory he had fought a good fight. The Bible reminds us that we are overcome by the blood of the Lamb. Amen.

# HE ALWAYS HEARS OUR PRAYERS
## Part 1

Does God respond to my moment of prayer? According to Isaiah 65:24, I wondered how long I must talk with Him for Him to answer me, not only long but how structured or orderly must these sentences be. In my youthful years, I recalled the fearful words directed to me by an elderly deacon,. saying God will not answer my prayer unless I was kneeling. As a typical naive youth, willing not only to listen to the counsel of my seniors but also to respect and acknowledge it as truth, I acknowledge what I was told. But it was troubling to me, nonetheless, wondering what if I'm being pursued by a ferocious animal, screaming for help not being able to assume a prayer posture, and God will not answer my prayer. Of course, as I grew older, I realized that was far from the truth. For example, on a cold December day, I encountered a patch of ice on the interstate. As traffic started to build up, I gently touched my brake, and the next thing I saw was my trailer looping around to my right, then to my left, and gently into a jackknife mode. At that time speakers on my CB radio were blasting, "He did it. He's done. He's done." By impulse, I shouted, "Jesus! Jesus!"

With a fifty-three-foot trailer dancing from left to right, there was no time for our so-called prayer posture or pray attitude, no time now to address Him as the God of Abraham, Isaac, and Jacob. I recall, as a young man getting ready to be active in church, that when I am scheduled to pray for a particular program, I would be given days' notice so that I can be prepared to pray. Do you think anything is inherently wrong with that? Not for a moment, however, there are times that when we are faced with an emergency, we will not be able to kneel, much less to consider a structured prayer. Because of your relationship with Him, He understands your every word regardless of how structured the sentences are. You see in almost every congregation, there are those who are known for the eloquent and coveted gift of praying, so when others are plagued by issues, they lose no time reaching out to what we now call prayer warriors—we say they can petition God in our behalf. While nothing is inherently wrong with that, but I think God enjoys it when we are in touch with Him personally. That day when I shouted Jesus! Jesus! There were no other words that followed. But something happened right then. There is power in the name of Jesus. There is healing in the name of Jesus. There is salvation in the name of Jesus, and if He allows me to attach a line, I will say that there was protection in the name of Jesus, there is restoration in the name of Jesus, and there is redirection in the name of Jesus. Imagine if asked to pray one day in your church and the one appointed to do so simply said, Jesus! Jesus! Jesus! Amen. It is unlikely that such a prayer will be affirmed by any portion of the congregation. In fact, many will remain on their knees or in their preferred posture waiting for the conclusion as they are accustomed to. With that one word Jesus, no English professor will acknowledge that as a complete sentence. No professor or any Bible college will accept that as a structured prayer. But when you have a relationship, a bond, an affinity with Jesus, like a mom with her infant, that mom knows well how to interpret that toddler's cry. She knows it's a cry for food, or, it might be a cry indicating an experience of discomfort. Depending on the tone of voice, mom knows exactly what's taking place, and when she gets that call, she responds accordingly. So our loving Savior, who was touched by the feelings of our infirmities, knows exactly our needs when He hears "Jesus." He knows exactly what the needs are, be it a physical or a financial situation or a memory of painful pasts. He knows it and how to respond; therefore, be not despair on account of not being able to assume a posture or do a structured prayer. Romans chapter 8 reminds us that even in our scheduled prayer, we don't know how to pray as we ought; it's the Holy Spirit that teaches us how to pray. In your moments of distress and agony, be it an emergency or a protracted condition. You need not give Him a long preamble, just one solitary word, or at times you might just be able to moan or groan. I assure you, the Spirit understands every thought and feeling of your heart that you wish to express, He then transforms it into a heavy language and presents them in your behalf at the Father's throne .

With the trailer sliding toward my right window, I had not a second to eloquently express my fears and my thoughts, but because I knew Him, I knew the master understands my inner longings, my needs, my desires, and my fears. I need not enumerate them in chronological order. He desires daily communion with me. He wants to talk with me while I'm walking, while I'm driving, and while I'm waiting to sign a document; He wants to hear from me. I promise you, practice having a daily conversation with Jesus! Meditate on His promises. You will be amazed at the love relationship between you and Jesus. You will feel a tightening bond and an affinity between yourself and your Savior so that you need not be doubtful as to whether He will listen to you only when you assume a certain posture.

# MYSTERIOUS DISAPPEARANCE
# OF RECORDS
## Part 1

As I think of Proverbs 21:1, God continues His mission of getting my attention by engaging in some strange struggle. I consider myself a reasonably outgoing person, so during my travels, I seize the opportunity to establish relationships with people from all walks of life. Given my activities across the nation, every so often I might need the services of one of these contacts. On this day in question, I attempted to renew my driver's license, but my home state denied me, claiming that the computer had rejected me due to an unresolved DMV matter in another state. I was fully aware of the matter and recall that it was settled over five years prior. The fact that I had not secured my receipt had placed me in a position of not being able to challenge it. At the close of business on that Friday, that northern state had confirmed the case status as being open and unresolved. I committed the matter to the Lord. I could not prove the previous payment, so I was ready for the consequences. I reached out with urgency to one of my friendly contacts in that region and diligently urged him to secure the record and settle the matter in my behalf. They were unable to locate the file on a Monday morning that was supposedly open and unresolved the Friday prior. They finally suggested to my power of attorney that it was probably sent across town to annex archives. While in conversation with the agency, my friend had placed the phone on the counter and allowed me to eavesdrop. I suggested that he queried whether they had a weekend staff assigned to archive their files(sarcastic). A diligent search in the archives proved futile, and the only recourse was to write me a statement of release. *What had occurred over the weekend? Did someone vandalize the office? Or better yet, because they no longer keep paper files, someone hacked the computer, or perhaps, he or she must have had unresolved departmental issues and may have destroyed records.* I recalled how I had spent that weekend thinking about how unfair the world is and how difficult it is to get justice from the system. I wrestled with the word of the song, "There's no abiding city here. We seek a city yet to come." As I thought of the song, this world is not my home. I'm just passing through, and the inequities will not last forever. But what brought peace and a level of solace to my soul was Psalm 119:165. I was now fully prepared to accept the Monday morning consequences following the Friday afternoon late conversation. The question to answer is what became of the records, not one but both states, had made the claim of unresolved cases. All I can say is, my God can do anything and will do it to deliver His children. Yes, He caused sounds of horsemen in the ears of Israel's antagonists that caused them to abandon camp and scatter, and He can do that and more for us today. Both states declared that they no longer had information of delinquency on my record. I had given the matter to the Lord, and He had a verdict. Oh, taste and see that the Lord is good; blessed is the man who trusts in Him.

# MYSTERIOUS DISAPPEARANCE OF RECORDS
## Part 2

Still on the matter of documents disappearing and unaccounted for. A newly constructed bridge had recently been opened to traffic, and in my haste on that day, I had not noticed the posted commercial truck restrictions. While crossing the bridge at the center span, I was in full sight of a trooper heading in the opposite direction. He immediately engaged his emergency lights seeking the opportunity for a U- turn. My heart skipped a beat because I knew he was in pursuit of me. My impulsive reaction was to take the first exit, but with other local and city commercial restrictions, who knows how much deeper I will sink into trouble. My final decision was to fabricate an excuse, but within moments, he had completed a U-turn was clear in my rearview that he was after me. I purposed in my heart not to allow that inner man to be resurrected and be in control. After assorting himself and displaying his authority, the result was, I was issued two citations. I made no plea for mercy, neither did I display hostility nor acts of defiance. I had decided to fully trust God. I was alone and reflecting on what had just transpired. I was inclined to lament. Perhaps I should have attempted an excuse or blamed someone for having done an improper maneuver that caused me to be in the left lane on the bridge. I thought I could have at least complained that the reason for my speed was that I had been rushing to create a safe distance between the vehicles that had been following me too closely. My mind was now becoming a battlefield, and thoughts from the enemy were now flashing in and out of my mind, but the Lord had already empowered me to surrender. I reflected on my previous encounters and how the Lord had dealt with me. It takes power to surrender, but you are empowered when you do. At about that time, an associate of mine caught my attention on my CB radio as he traveled in the opposite direction. He went on to explain that the officer had been having a field day at that location issuing citations to commercial vehicles and that the courts in that jurisdiction are often merciless. In fact, he explained that the courts are known to issue penalties on commercial vehicles beginning from two thousand dollars, claiming that he knows someone who was cited for this similar infraction and his penalty was two thousand dollars plus points.

With urgency, I reached out to my commercial driver's license association and restored my delinquent membership and allowed them to resolve this matter. I feared not only the exorbitant fine, but the five points minimum that is assessed on the driver's license. I was told some time ago that there is a protocol for getting some jurisdiction not to access points on one's profile, that is, mail the ticket immediately with a reasonable amount covering fees and court costs. I did that, and anxious weeks went by without a response while negative thoughts flashed in and out of my mind. *Did I mail it to a proper address? Did I post a return address?* Sure, enough after several long torturous weeks slipped by, one day I received a reasonably thick envelope from the state in question. I nervously opened it and recognize they had returned my letter, the citation, and my check with a note reading "No such citation was found in our system." I was dumbfounded and proceeded to inquire from my driver's club whether they had dealt with the ticket. To my amazement, they too had not gotten a response from the court. *Can God do it? Is anything too hard for Him?* He has

47

thousands of ways that we know not of to deliver His children. It's best when we acknowledge our sins and humble ourselves before Jehovah. Is it not true that He is intimately involved in our daily lives and is interested in the minutest things that concern us? I have been shamed too often because of my impulsive and feeble excuses in my efforts to defuse matters of this sort. The songwriter says, "Oh what peace we often forfeit. Oh, what needless pain we bear all because we do not carry everything, yes, everything to God in prayer. For His ways are past finding out."

When He washes your sins away, they are completely removed. No devil in hell can recognize it; He leaves no residue nor stains. If He can delete all records from the archives or from a national computer for me, I know He can do it for you also, but most of all, He can delete your sins.

Therefore, anything negative that may have followed you in your personal life, in your heart, whether depressing thoughts or guilt hindering your progress, I promise you, Jesus can delete them all and give you a clean page and a new start.

# MIRACULOUS DELIVERANCE

The Angel of the Lord encamped round about them that fear Him. As I talked about God's ability to protect, my mind goes back to a snowy day in the Midwestern states. I had almost crested a hill when I noticed a disabled tractor-trailer jackknifed in my path. The icy road condition will not allow me to engage my brakes, and with very little room to squeeze by on the right shoulder, I took that as my best option. With very little room to coordinate my maneuver through that path, my fear was that given the icy road condition, chances are that any slight wind can move my vehicle, thus making it difficult or impossible to navigate through what was already a narrow path. Once again, no time for a structured prayer or to assume a praying posture and not enough time to call my family to inform them of a possible major collision. All this was happening in a matter of seconds. Then came the moment. I guided the tractor slowly but skillfully through the narrow path with the guardrail on my right and the jackknifed truck on my left, but it was just too narrow, and before I knew it, with a tremendous jerk, my tractor was bound between the guardrail and the disabled jackknifed tractor. With fear and anxiety and thinking about the worst possible thing, I knew I was consciously shouting Jesus! Jesus! Within seconds, I felt another impact on the left; it was so severe, and it scattered much of my belongings in my sleeper as well as in the cab. By now I was shouting at the top of my lungs, "Jesus, help me! Jesus, help me!" I was conscious enough to stand and shake myself off hoping that all was well with me, but I was rudely slumped to the floor due to another severe impact on my right. Terror and fear were not crippling me because I was aware that other vehicles were piling up on my rear. Adrenaline was now in full control.

I was able to grab my briefcase and exited my vehicle while still slightly disoriented. As I began to examine this scene, I noticed I was one of five semis and two cars that had choked the interstate. I could not be more graphic for fear of reawakening emotions. Following the investigation, all injured parties were escorted to the emergency rooms while wreckers were scrambling to tow the damaged and disabled vehicles to a temporary salvage yard. But the surprise of the day was, my trailer had sustained the impact mainly at the rear end, and I was able to drive to the nearest truck stop. In fact, two of the trucks involved in the wreckage were my friends, so we ended up sleeping in my truck for the rest of that night. It was an astonishing sight to witness one of seven vehicles driving away such wreckage. It troubled law enforcement that I was driving to the truck stop, and I recalled they trailed me in the interest of public safety.

Do I need to repeat once again, angels of the Lord encamped round about them that fear Him? Some call Him the Rose of Sharon, others say He is a bright morning star. Ezekiel describes Him as the wheel in a wheel. For me He is a deliverer, a protector, a forgiver, a grace supplier, a present help in a time of need, and a persistent and relentless seeker. He is a big truck navigator. Yes, I can attest to it. I am a living proof, and my life is a testimony of who He is. I actually experience it all. These are not simply lyrics; they are descriptions of my experience, and no devil in hell can undermine this conviction. It is edged indelibly in my mind, and I know that God is pursuing me for His purpose. So I submit daily afresh to Him that I know His will, and He gives me the courage to obey.

# VICTORY THROUGH SURRENDERING

The Bible is replete with verses that speak about the idea of overcoming—overcoming any condition that haunted you and control you, preventing you from experiencing the vibrant Christian experience and living the life of a transformed being. This might be the most challenging testimony to share as well as the most transparent, but the Spirit insisted that I do it because it's not about me but, it's about the healing or restoration of others.

When I first came to this country, I spent several years in New York prior to relocating South. It was a hot summer day in Brooklyn, and at age twenty-seven, it was my first experience sitting through a pornographic movie. My cousin had protected this piece of equipment securely hiding it in the house. Living in New York, countertop magazine and posters of a pornographic nature are a common sight, but to sit and be entertained by such suggestive material allow the subject matter to penetrate the mind at a deeper level. The truth was, one side of me had been absorbing and feasting on the material, but in the end, I was overwhelmed with remorse and shame, and I entreated the Lord to erase or delete them from my memory. My busy schedule did not afford me to ponder on it, and it never reoccurred.

Almost twenty years had passed, and I had relocated to the South and into a ministry that was very uplifting where I always enjoyed my quiet and meditative movement. On this day, I was entering a store to pay for my fuel, my attention was drawn to a shed with a poster that read "adult only." I know it's difficult for you to believe that I did not discern the subtle message on that poster. My interest was aroused, and my feet effortlessly made their way to that reserved area, and immediately I was mesmerized by the pornographic magazine and tapes. I recalled browsing through and before long I had armed myself with a one-hour tape and headed down the road. The time was just about noon, and my ETA was close to midnight, but along the way for the next four hours, my thoughts were consumed by the pleasure I anticipated in viewing that video. My earlier New York encounter had been mentally resurrected, and now I was fully controlled by that awakened desire. It was now dark, and the time and atmosphere were conducive to such immoral behavior. I chose a rest area that was very quiet and then carefully inserted my video and immersed my mind and spirit in a world of pornography for one full hour. Surely, it satisfied my carnal mind. I was enthralled. My imagination was wide and deep and very intense, and I was hypnotized and glued to my screen. The movie had ended, and this screen appeared black, and the words appeared in bold letters, THE END. It's as though my body was frozen. I know I wanted to move, but there was no strength in my body to perform the act because my mind was deeply confused and started to add words to the phrase I had last seen on the video, the end. My added words were (of time), thus making the sentence THE END OF TIME. As a Christian anticipating the sure return of the Messiah, and when time on earth will cease, can you imagine my state of mind during those moments? The end of time. There were thoughts such as for all those years gone by that you were never honest and your prayers were not in harmony with God. You were simply deceiving yourself, and there is no need to keep on trying. Intellectually, I know that the life of a Christian is a battle and a march, but the enemy had succeeded in convincing me that my walk with God was over. Those moments were agonizing and seemed like they lasted forever before I was finally able to compose myself and commence driving. The remaining hours of my journey were very painful, overwhelmed with shame and anguish. It seemed like the distance between each mile post had gotten longer. I longed for time to pass away, and that the event of the last few hours be forever behind me. After mustering the strength and the courage to ask forgiveness, I recognized that it was a very important act on my part but had to be done. I thought of Joshua 7:13, "I could not win the battle. I could not overcome until I put away the accursed thing from my midst." When the Spirit brought this fact to my mind, I hastened to the nearest dumpster, and with disdain, I angrily disposed of it. Sometimes we join in the chorus and sing, "All to Jesus I surrender, all to Him I freely give." We often do it just because we are directed by the worship leader and we follow the congregation and sing, but we often fail to realize that there are things in our lives that we must get rid of as we sing of total surrender. We will never experience real victory and peace of mind until all has been surrendered. Thank God for His grace forgiveness and His redeeming power. I accepted the forgiveness of Jesus and continued my walk with Him. Sometimes I wish that Christians will be persistent and determined to walk with the Lord just as persistent and determined as the enemy is to trip us up. Why did I expect that the devil will not confront me again with the same weapon? That event was off my radar and out of the clear blue skies; the enemy had once again engaged me in battle. Notice this, the enemy does not attack unless he takes perfect aim. Unlike many Christians, we do not fish wisely for souls. We miss out on moments when we can plant seeds in the heart of men and women, times when it is more susceptible, when the ground is fertile, or when the hearts are yearning. It might be seasons of pagan custom and celebration, one that has crept into the Christian Church such as Easter or Christmas on December 25. But because we do not subscribe to these theological beliefs and holidays doesn't mean that it is off- season for us to fish for souls. I submit that many who show little or no interest in attending church regularly, will often adjust their calendars to accommodate attending a religious service and be ready to entertain conversation of a spiritual nature. The enemy, likewise, waits and assesses the times and seasons before he makes a deliberate attack, and very seldom does he miss.

On this day, I was among many drivers who had all suffered the same fate at the delivery location. On a scale from one to ten, my anger level was seven. I had no energy nor desire to relent especially because there were others with me having this similar frustration triggered by the same incident. We all had decided to retreat to a nearby restaurant and neutralize our anger. Sure enough, a section in that restaurant was dedicated to pornographic material, what a perfect environment to calm the Spirit and subdue the emotion. Before long we were all feasting with our eyes and our minds, and the occasional loud outburst was an indication that someone had come across the most sensual picture or scene. It lasted for a while, and I don't recall anyone having purchased a sandwich as intended. That's what I mean by the need for Christian persistence and my statement about Christians needing to seize the moment to fish for souls. That's exactly what the enemy had done—seized the moment.

Almost one year had passed since the previous encounter of its kind. (Remember, I promise transparency.) I have not been thinking along those lines at all. I didn't expect the enemy to attack me at least so quickly after he had lost the previous battle. But inasmuch as he is unflagging and furious in his attack, he's also patient and waits for the opportune time to launch his missiles. I was already angry, so angry with no time to be rational;, the atmosphere was contaminated and well- suited for the enemy to operate. I found myself walking back toward my truck with my newly released video; suddenly my steps became arduous, and my mind was confused. Then it dawned on me, or rather, when I came to my senses, I asked, "What have I done?" Those four words tortured my mind for hours. It was reported that one of the pilots in the cockpit of the Hiroshima attack, after having seen the devastation he had caused, declared, "What have we done?" That was kind of how I felt about my actions after making such a purchase. I felt that I had betrayed myself, but most of all, I was crushed in my spirit, knowing that I had once more betrayed my Jesus who had done so much for me during those years and brought me through many previous challenges, and now I had done this again like a dog returning to its vomit, helpless. Guilt and despair had begun to sit in. I questioned whether I can be free from this reprehensible vile and sinful act that I had once again committed. I sat for a while and wallow in my misery, feeling incarcerated and almost lifeless, and then Jesus stepped in. He brought me to my knees to acknowledge and confess. I sought forgiveness and move on. He brought to my mind Proverbs 24:16 at that moment. I felt a release, my burden was lifted, and a sense of reassurance rushed through my spirit, and things were not the same. I had acknowledged my weakness and my inability to change my condition by myself. I had asked Him for the courage to accept His forgiveness and be ready to move forward. But the accursed object was still in my vehicle, and for me to move on, it was imperative that I dispose of all disgustingly objectionable material. Unlike my previous encounter with the video that I had trashed into a dumpster, I recognized that to get certain results I had never gotten before, I had to do some things I had never done before. On this occasion, I elected to set the video on the ground and deliberately rolled my eighteen-wheeler back and forth with seventy-five thousand pounds gross weight on it to the extent that it was no longer recognizable.

When God forgives, He cleanses, He makes the page clean, and His blood washes so the enemy can no longer recognize your sins. I recognize that on my part. I had to be decisive and deliberate in my acts. Crushing the tape, that action was of major significance to me. There was no vestige of it to be seen, no possibility of anyone salvaging or rescuing it from the dump, and from that day on, glory be to God I've never again been trapped by that recalcitrant and transgressive behavior.

Victory! My friends, the Bible did not mask the imperfections of any of its characters. Their multitude of heinous sins and inequities are clearly chronicled, and their tremendous and sometimes shameful failures, as well as their struggles to overcome, are all highlighted. There were many from the lowly walk of life as well as many who can trace their beginning as from a strong religious background, and many have had regrettable and sometimes shameful past, but those who gained the victory were those who deliberately decided to go that extra mile. Therefore, fight like you have never fought before. I'm thinking of one who said "I die daily," daily so that as the enemy throws missiles at his body, it will do him no harm. That same character declared, "I have fought a good fight," not someone throwing punches in the air but punches that connect on the opponent. "I have kept the faith," he said, "henceforth there is a crown laid up for me." There are more battles to be fought and more victories to win. Remember , he that overcomes will I grant to sit with Me on my Father's throne (Rev. 3:21 KJV). You will share in His glory He says just as He shared in His Father's glory (Rev. 2:7). We are admonished to overcome; it requires action. It is as we overcome with God's help that we will gain victory. There are blessings promised to those who overcome, and God has provisions for us so that we can overcome. There's a crown for all who will overcome. Keep fighting, stand on his promises, hold on to the horns of the altar, hold on to your faith in God, and hold on tenaciously and unflinchingly. Never give up hope, for He who has promised is faithful. Keep fighting, keep fighting, keep fighting. See you in glory! Amen.

The End

# ABOUT THE AUTHOR

Edward has vivid memories of the church services that were held in his home up to the age of thirteen. As the son of a preacher, he lived by the teachings and principles of the Seventh-Day Adventist denomination. The death of his father marked the beginning of a time in his youth during which his relationship with God was inconsistent. In his late teens, he consciously recommitted and renewed his walk with Christ. After marrying at the age of twenty-three, he started a family. Although Edward never attended any private or parochial schools as a child, he worked to ensure that his children would have the opportunity to attend Seventh-Day Adventist schools.

Most of his adult life was spent serving in his local churches with roles ranging from youth director to senior elder and even serving on the executive committee of the regional church conference. Despite his belief that his destiny lay with evangelism, circumstances were such that any formal training could not bring this to fruition. However, this did not dampen Edward's passion for kingdom business.

Relocating to Florida to provide his children with a less hectic environment, his career shifted to that of a long-distance trucker. During his extensive travels across the United States and Canada, he encountered people from all walks of life and found himself in situations that should have ended his life. Edward's experiences over the last thirty years as a commercial long-distance driver revealed to him a truth he could no longer deny: God was working directly in his life. Through these experiences and the periods of self-reflection, he came to know that his birth as a second-generation Adventist or service in the church would not earn him a place in God's kingdom. He knew that God was setting him up and preparing him for a purpose that was beyond his wildest dreams. The testimonies shared here are a striking example of what can happen when one surrenders completely to God.